PHOTOGRAPHY
in America's National Parks

Contents

A little over three years ago a decision was made to embark on a major photographic undertaking: to photograph, using the best photographers and equipment available, the outstanding beauty, grandeur and fascination of America's national parks.

As everyone knows, the United States of America constitute a vast area of dramatically changing landscape and climate; from the frozen reaches of Alaska to the steaming swamplands of the Florida Everglades; from the volcanic islands of Hawaii with their palm-fringed beaches to the arid depths of the Grand Canyon in Arizona and, situated as they are in all parts of the country, the national parks exemplify these extremes.

The task, then, was formidable. Different times of the year provide ideal photographic conditions in different parks and although weather is not completely predictable anywhere in the world, expected conditions had to be taken into account when planning the photography, together with contingency plans that had to be made to ensure that if conditions proved untypical, and impossible for photography, in one location, the photographer could be switched, with the minimum delay and disruption, to a new location.

For such an undertaking, forward planning of all detail is essential. Hotels, for instance, are out of the question in some locations. A photographer may need to start shooting at dawn, or continue through the day and into the late evening to get the effects he wants, and meals and sleeping arrangements have to be adjusted in accordance with his schedule. He needs a huge supply of film plus, particularly when working in high temperatures, some form of refrigeration. Equipment breakdowns, and with so much modern equipment being battery dependent, battery failures, have to be considered to the extent that almost every item of equipment must be backed up by other, similar items, and all batteries require spares—and spares for the spares! All of this, plus clothing and personal items has, needless to say, to be carried.

Accordingly, campers were bought and equipped and the team of photographers—Edmund Nägele F.R.P.S., Neil Sutherland, Nick Meers, William Curwen, Eberhard Streichan and Peter Beney—were flown to various parts of the United States, to collect them and start work.

It would be satisfying to be able to say, truthfully, that everything went exactly according to plan; that there were no problems, and that the job was finished smoothly and simply. Life, however, seldom works out like that—and hardly ever on photographic trips! Of course there were problems. Equipment *did* break down and film stocks, however carefully planned, *did* run short—and both had to be airlifted or, in a few cases, bought locally. Unseasonal weather conditions *were* encountered and it proved impossible, at times, to switch photographers to other locations—in which case there was nothing to be done but to sit things out and wait for conditions to improve. And of course it was all extremely expensive.

Having said that, it is, nevertheless, to the great credit of all the photographers—their tenacity, determination, expertise, professionalism—call it what you will, that an outstanding collection of color transparencies was produced, matching the sheer beauty and magnificence of the subjects the photographers were sent to photograph. In many ways the photographers were hugely privileged. They were witness, at first hand, to scenes that many of us only dream of, and they all have a rich store of memories and experiences to recall.

It is not possible, within the confines of just one book, to show more than a representative selection of the photographs taken, but those that do appear surely provide ample evidence of the successful accomplishment of a difficult, albeit rewarding, task.

David Gibbon
Creative Director.
Library International Ltd.

Introduction

While this book was being compiled, Mount St. Helens in the State of Washington erupted. "The gods are angry in the Cascades," the *New York Times* headlined. Indeed, it has been an awesome experience. To a nation that annually loses lives and property in staggering figures, the power of St. Helens has been mind-shattering. And the best predictions are that it could be years before the volcano finally rests.

This is the first volcanic eruption in the continental United States since Mount Lassen, 400 miles to the south in California, exploded in 1914 and 1915. Probably no worse in its destruction than Lassen, Mount St. Helens has been a media event, to put it in electronic-age parlance. Virtually every rumble of the earth, every belch of steam and ash, has been reported to the world, sometimes within minutes of its happening. No other volcano in history has received such global attention. And yet somewhere between the tragic loss of precious lives and valuable timberlands and the selling of souvenir ash for a dollar on the streets of Seattle, the real significance of what has taken place has been overshadowed.

Mount St. Helens has told us — perhaps reminded us is better — tragically, yet so vividly, that all is not yet done on this earth. The Colorado River slowly grinds away at the floor of the Grand Canyon, and at Bryce and Zion and Arches and the Canyonlands of Utah, the winds and rains inexorably carve and slice the landscape, but here the processes are exceedingly slow and these places have become attractions of beauty where changes are barely perceived from one generation to the next. But suddenly on Sunday, May 18, 1980, in one mighty burst of nature that, according to experts, equaled 500 times the force of the atomic bomb dropped on Hiroshima, the earth moved and within hours had significantly altered more than 150 square miles of the planet and affected thousands more beyond.

It was not exactly without warning that St. Helens blew. The last recorded series of eruptions began in 1831 and lasted for twenty-five years, all when the land was sparsely populated and communications to the outside world non-existent. And then all was quiet. But in 1978, just two years in advance, two U.S. Geological Survey volcanologists wrote: "In the future, Mount St. Helens probably will erupt violently and inter-mittently just as it has in the recent geologic past, and these future eruptions will affect human life and health, property, agriculture and general economic welfare over a broad area."

When you stand by a Giant Sequoia or at the rim of the Grand Canyon or at the base of the Rocky Mountains, it is for but a second on the great calendar of time, and one thinks that here time has stopped, that the trees, the rivers, the mountains have always been like this and they always will be. It's difficult to envisage the natural processes that created these things, the processes that are still going on. There has been little change in the Grand Canyon since John Wesley Powell first explored the Colorado; the big trees still grow yet they have not significantly altered in appearance since first discovered; and the mountains move beneath the surface without much to jar our security.

But John Muir, standing atop the California Sierras, understood. "The last days of this glacial winter are not yet past, so young is our world," he wrote. "I used to envy the father of our race, dwelling as he did in contact with the new-made fields and plants of Eden; but I do so no more, because I have discovered that I also live in creation's dawn; the morning stars still sing together, and the world, not yet half-made, becomes more beautiful every day."

Mount St. Helens is but the latest manifestation of "creation's dawn"; and "a world not yet half-made". It goes on right before our eyes. Recently, following scenes of the Grand Canyon, a television commentator graphically remarked: "And if you don't fix that leak in the outside faucet, that's what your backyard will look like in a couple of million years."

Mount St. Helens is not a national park, although it may be someday. Within a few weeks following the first eruption there was talk among the powers in Washington that the U.S. Forest Service, under whose domain the mountain and its timberland had been administered, would offer it to the National Park Service. Even President Carter, following his visit to the disaster area, hinted at new economic possibilities in the volcano and its environs. "People will come from all over the world to observe the impressiveness of the force of nature...it would be...a tourist attraction that would equal the Grand Canyon."

The President's words did little to encourage the devastated people of the Northwest, and no doubt National Park Service officials cringed at the mammoth responsibilities of administering, protecting, and interpreting the volcano as a National Park. Yet this could be. This is what the National Park Service is all about, and if such is the mandate of the United States Congress, Mount St. Helens will pass into the hands of the best and most experienced organization in the world to preserve this geologic phenomenon for the future.

Without doubt controversy will rage over St. Helens — preservation for its scientific importance and/or for the "pleasure" of the people. Exponents of both will be at loggerheads, one arguing that the mountain cannot be trampled by anyone but scientists, the other saying the public must have an opportunity to see, experience, enjoy. The fact is that both will win out in the end, for this too is what national parks are all about.

John Muir wrote in 1898: "Thousands of nerveshaken, overcivilized people are beginning to find out that going to the mountains is going home; that wilderness is a necessity; and that mountain parks and reservations are useful not only as fountains of timber and irrigating rivers, but as fountains of life." Muir was talking about the Yosemites and Sequoias and Yellowstones, but were he alive today, without question he would support the preservation of Mount St. Helens as a "fountain of knowledge".

There are 322 areas in the National Park Service, a total of some seventy-six million acres of the United States set aside for the public. Forty of these areas are designated National Parks; all but one, Mesa Verde, representing the most significant natural features of the North American continent. These are, in the truest sense, America's national treasures; perhaps more importantly they are treasures belonging to the world, a modern-day calendar upon which we measure the earth, our tenancy on it, and, if we perceive it correctly, the future. Virtually every acre of the forty parks, including Mesa Verde, is inexorably linked to the passage of time and the fragile, unsure thread of tomorrow.

The spectacles of Acadia, the Everglades, Mount McKinley, the Badlands...they all belie the turmoil which orchestrated their beginnings as national parks. In fact, one must marvel that they exist at all. But for a handful of farsighted individuals, names most Americans would not readily recognize, we would not see, let alone ever really understand, how this land was formed, how it appeared in its original state, the role nature has played in our lives. These were men of vision who saw and held fast to their convictions, and, ultimately, set a course of preservation that would extend to the far reaches of the globe.

That America pioneered the national park idea is true. That it all began solely as an effort to preserve the country's natural beauty and resources is doubtful, and we live under no illusions. But after more than a century of national parks, the early motives are immaterial. It makes little difference how they began. The treasures are ours and it will forever be a mark on mankind how they are preserved.

The beauty and diversity of scenery in the United States of America is highlighted in the country's National Parks. These protected areas are a haven for wildlife, and an oasis of peace and tranquillity for the thousands of people who visit them each year. The Grand Canyon opposite is possibly the most famous natural wonder in the world.

Acadia

Sunrise touches the United States first here at Acadia National Park in Maine, a place where, in contrast to the delicate morning light and the surrounding, soft fingers of fog, the irresistible sea clashes harshly with an immovable, rocky coastline. By comparison, Acadia is one of the smaller national parks, but its size makes it no less important in the chain of great natural areas held in preservation by the nation. As a matter of fact, it is the size that makes it such a special place: the last vestige of the "rock-bound coast of Maine". There is really nothing quite like it along the Atlantic and no other place in the East where the geological story is so closely linked to glaciers and the sea.

First established as Lafayette National Park in 1919, Acadia, renamed in 1929, was the first national park in the East and the only one in New England. The boundaries are as jagged as the shore, but this is a park that has grown and developed from within.

There are other primitive areas here in the East and in the West, but there is something special about Acadia.

Maine's National Park is Acadia, where the cold Atlantic waters meet rocky coastline, with craggy cliffs and beautiful beaches. The area is strewn with lighthouses and fortresses, and timber-clad buildings, all carefully preserved and restored, to illustrate, and remind future generations of their heritage.

New England is justly famous for its spectacularly colorful Fall. Thickly-forested areas glow with rich reds, burnished browns, golden yellows and brilliant oranges— reflected against a bright blue sky, a glorious example of natural beauty.

Arches & Canyonlands

Utah, Arizona, New Mexico, Colorado. Four Corners. The Colorado Plateau. The land of canyons.

The Colorado Plateau is an island of flat-lying rock between the Rocky Mountains and the deserts of the West: a high, flat table, dotted here and there with isolated snow-capped peaks and laced with an interconnecting, rugged and dramatic scenery that sweeps the mind with shapes and colors. This is nature's hideaway, seemingly forbidden to man and beast alike. Water created this plateau, and it is water that has eaten into its heart and slowly, inexorably taken it away. Nowhere is this erosion more dramatically demonstrated than in the southeast corner of Utah at Arches and Canyonlands National Parks.

The mighty Colorado River, flowing from the east, meets its tributary, the Green River, flowing from the north, in the heart of Canyonlands National Park. Together they shape, as they have done longer than man knows, the most incredible examples of water erosion on the earth; there's nothing like it anywhere. And it is a monstrous task to describe. "I

Arches National Park lies in the heart of Utah and contains more natural stone arches, windows, spires and pinnacles than anywhere else in the country. Top right *shows South Park Avenue;* bottom right *is the majestic Double Arch.*

North window provides a perfect frame for Turret Arch in the background right, *while South Window is seen* above right. Below *Brightly colored flowers front The Organ; The Garden of Eden* above is *highlighted against a bright blue sky, its strange formations soaring above the rocky terrain.*

Arches & Canyonlands

would describe Canyonlands as the place where the adjective died from exhaustion", wrote Freeman Tilden. He was right. Even those who attempted to name the formations relied on the noun: Bagpipe Butte, Elephant Canyon, Devil's Lane, The Sewing Machine, The Doll House. There are arches, pillars, needles, spires, pinnacles, domes, steeples, and hundreds of others that need only the eye and a vivid imagination. Massive sandstone columns stand like skyscrapers. Angel Arch has an opening 190 feet high under which could sit the Arc de Triomphe, with

some 16 feet to spare. And some of this is still unexplored.

The scenery in Arches National Park, just to the north of Moab and only a short distance from Canyonlands, is every bit as spectacular. This small park — small in comparision to Canyonlands, but huge in its array of geological formations — lies on the north bank of the Colorado River as it passes into Utah. Here is a phenomenal collection of natural arches, windows, spires, rocks balanced precariously on rocks — the most concentrated assemblage in the country.

Late afternoon sun emphasizes the glowing colors of the rock above on the trail near Peekaboo Spring. Two of the many impressive formations are Squaw Flat below, in the Needles District, and Angel Arch below left, found at the end of Salt Creek Trail. Shown from the Grand View Point of Island in the Sky, the scene top right gives some indication of the vast scale of this geological wonder.

Salt Creek drains a large part of The Needles district of Canyonlands, making its way into the Colorado River just northeast of that river's meeting with the Green River. The Creek has carved its way through the rock, creating sights like those shown these pages.

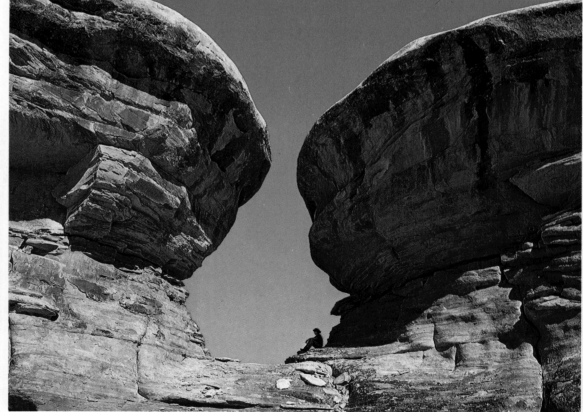

The fascinating petroglyphs right have been carved in the blackened surface of Newspaper Rock to reveal the clean sandstone underneath, probably over a period covering 1,000 years. What they do not reveal is how the Anasazi people managed to survive in such an inhospitable area.

Arches & Canyonlands

Right *The vastness of the entrance to Joint Trail, leading to Chester Park, is illustrated by the figure of a man. Below is just one of the many plants which have gained a foothold in this remarkable southeast corner of Utah. The Indian paintbrush, a member of the figwort family, provides a welcome splash of color with its bright orange-red blossom.*

The stark features and monuments of Canyonlands National Park are perfectly silhouetted against the gold of a setting sun. Pictured from Big Spring Canyon Overlook opposite page bottom, *figures lend scale to the huge rock formations, while North and South Sixshooter Peaks are shown* above.

The Flats, near Canyon Overlook, are pictured far left, *while The Wooden Show* left *provides a background for a profusion of western peppergrass, a member of the mustard family.*

Big Bend

Nestled in the arid, rugged, and forbidding great curve of the Rio Grande in southwest Texas, Big Bend is a lesson in true solitude where man meets the conflicting forces of nature and wonders how anyone… anything has survived. This is a land of incredible heat and freezing cold, virtually without rainfall, yet blooming with life, high mountains and basins, great distances and microscopic life, gentle beauty amid desolate surroundings, brooding silences and the lilting song of a wren…it is all this and much more…endless space, endless time on the horizons of America's frontier.

Like much of southwest Texas, Big Bend country was under shallow seas millions of years ago. As the continent heaved this way and that, some of this land was exposed and great swamps grew, harboring dinosaurs and huge, winged reptiles. And then the continent shifted again, this time pushing up the Rockies and the Sierra Madres. Here the Chisos Mountains sprang up between the two. Thousands of years later the Rio Grande began to carve its way through this mass of twisted rock. Now it seems to be the only living thing to have survived.

The last great wilderness area of Texas, Big Bend National Park these pages is a popular recreation area, with miles of trails available for hiking and horse-back riding; and rivers and lakes for canoeing and fishing.

Big Bend is essentially a park for those with a real love of the outdoors and for such people it can hardly be bettered. Modern civilization and all its trappings—and pressures—can be left far behind and a simple basic way of life enjoyed.

There are numerous information plaques in the park, and there are rules that have to be observed, often for the visitors' own safety.

Overleaf: *A lone canoeist makes his way through spectacular scenery; towering canyon walls reflect the sunlight which shimmers on the gray-green water.*

The primitive country of Big Bend National Park has been called hazardous and untameable, and there is no doubt that it can be very inhospitable, yet, as the pictures these pages *show, it possesses a* lonely, rugged and stark grandeur as well as much beauty, and it can certainly serve to rekindle our sense of adventure. The colorful sunset above *provides a perfect background for Big Bend's unforgettable terrain.*

Natural monuments jut into blue sky, from harsh, unfriendly terrain. Yet Big Bend, like many other desert areas, can burst into flower, covering the ground with a carpet of exotically-colored blooms, and creating a brilliant landscape.

Bryce Canyon

Bryce Canyon, established as a national park in 1928, is not really a canyon at all. Unlike nearby Zion, which is the canyon of the Virgin River, Bryce is the side of a plateau of varying kinds of stone that simply melted or washed away. Almost exclusively, water has been the erosive agent at Bryce, water in the form of heavy rains and snow and ice. It is more a washing process than cutting or carving as in the Grand Canyon.

There seems to have been some uplifting and tilting going on in Utah millions of years ago, leaving great plateaus that form a natural staircase, so to speak, from Bryce southwest to the Grand Canyon. These plateaus, separated by the mighty forces of rivers, are all different in composition, and it is that composition, layer upon layer of sediment deposited when this land was all part of a great inland sea, that not only gave them their colors and names, but determined the erosion after-math. There are the Chocolate Cliffs of Arizona at the Grand Canyon; working north are the Vermilion Cliffs, then the White Cliffs, the Gray Cliffs, and at Bryce, the Pink Cliffs. The brilliant Pink Cliffs are about 54 million years old and about 9,000 feet above sea level. The Kaibab limestone of the Grand Canyon is 225 million years old and about 2,500 feet above sea level.

The rock formations in all of these great chasms are intitially dependent on the kind of sediment laid down. Fresh water lakes covered the Bryce area leaving a very fine-grained and soft siltstone and a slightly harder limestone. Sprinkled throughout are thin layers of shale. All of these erode at a different rate, thus the variety of shapes and sizes of formations. Bryce Canyon is really two parks: the high, forested plateau and the beautiful scenery below.

The colorful, and quite incredible formations in Bryce Canyon are the result of rocks, shale and sandstone which have all eroded at different rates, allowing the elements to create fantastic sculptures and free-standing columns. The pictures these pages were taken on and around the Queen's Garden Trail.

Paria View overleaf is seen against a moonlit sky. From this vantage point, the landscape rolls away for mile after mile until it reaches the distant horizon.

Paria View is pictured again above, *this time in bright sunshine, while shadow covers part of Navajo Loop, seen from Sunset Point* above right, *and* above far right *riders follow the Peekaboo Trail, with the Wall of Windows in the background.*

Some of the formations in Bryce Canyon seem more the products of fantasy than of nature, like Balanced Rock left. *Heavy storm clouds gather at Inspiration Point* right, *where Gothic-looking spires and turrets fill the canyon floor.*

Capitol Reef

The word "fold" is probably the best to use for a description of Capitol Reef. It was the most recent dramatic upheaval here and took place some sixty million years ago. Before that, say back 250 million years, the Capitol Reef geological story began with a shallow sea covering much of the Colorado Plateau. For the next nearly 200 million years this land heaved and sighed a dozen times, drawing and collecting waters that alternately laid down strata of new materials and eroded them away.

The great folding took place about the time the Rocky Mountains were uplifted to the east. All of the Colorado Plateau was raised a little in this process, but here in south-central Utah the earth's crust wrinkled into a long S-shaped formation. There was other activity in the intervening years, and the evidence is here — boulders rounded from miles of rolling by water force, volcanic plugs from lava seeping into fissures — but for the most part it was eons of erosion that created this spectacular place. There seem to be no more cataclysmic upheavals in store for Capitol Reef but still melting snows, flash floods and torrential rains continue to wear and tear the landscape.

Situated between Bryce Canyon and Canyonlands National Parks, Capitol Reef contains many splendid natural monuments. Erosion is responsible for the graceful sweep of the Cassidy Arch right, *while* left *the Pectol Pyramid soars skywards.*

Above is Eph Hanks Tower, named for an early pioneer and leader in the Mormon Church, while left *is shown an unusual view of the feature known as Twin Rocks.*

Water, in its various forms, has caused the erosion seen in the photographs right *and* far right—*the diversity of shapes and formations is a major influence in creating Capitol Reef National Park.*

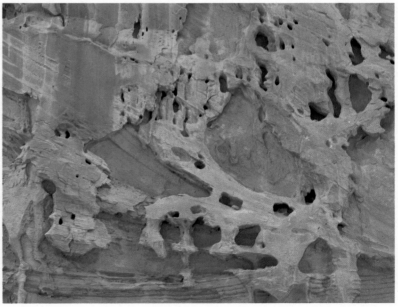

Capitol Reef

Far left *Chimney Rock towers over the surrounding landscape, capped by hard rock; the Egyptian Temple* above *is another example of the impressive structures found in Capitol Reef.* Left and opposite page below *These pictures illustrate further examples of the action of water on rock, creating strange contours.*

The Narrows left *are shown in their enormity against a group of men. Eking out a precarious living in the meagre soil of the area are claret cup cacti* above, *their bright flowers rich against the ground.*

Forming a perfect frame for an impressive view of the park beyond, is Hickman Natural Bridge overleaf, named for J. S. Hickman, a supporter for the preservation of Capitol Reef.

Carlsbad Caverns

A room with a ceiling twenty-five stories high and a floor of fourteen football fields — that's the Big Room of Carlsbad Caverns, the largest underground gallery of all the explored caves in the world.

Carlsbad Caverns' history goes back to something like 200 million years ago, when geologic forces and seas formed the nearby Guadalupe Mountains. Like in other underground yawnings, sediments were laid, bends and cracks occurred, waters filled and drained, and minerals seeped through. Millions of years in the making, the finished product, if indeed it is finished, carries a master's touch.

Carlsbad Caverns is beautiful. It is enormous and not yet completely explored. Seven miles of chambers and passageways are open; more exist that may lead into the Guadalupes — no one knows for certain. But those which one may visit are a wonderland of the weird; almost ghostly when specially lighted, columns standing at every turn.,.better still, they loom from the floor. Overhead hang stalactites in the shape of intricate chandeliers of frozen waterfalls; one spectacular ceiling formation is called the "Sword of Damocles." The Green Lake Room, the King's Palace, the Queen's Chambers…each little alcove and niche has its own special charm.

Structures like the Giant Dome and Twin Domes in the Hall of Giants far right in the Carlsbad Caverns, were created by droplets of water containing minute quantities of dissolved limestone which slowly formed the fantastic shapes we see today. In places the process still continues, but too slowly for us to observe during our lifetime.

Glorious colors highlight the strange formations.

Above *Glowing against the dark cavern walls is the Temple of the Sun.*

Shown these pages *is a selection taken from the many natural wonders in the vast, underground chambers of the Carlsbad Caverns, formed in a limestone reef by percolating ground water, beneath the rugged foothills of the Guadalupe Mountains. In this subterranean wonderland the huge galleries are filled with delicate stone formations, massive stalactites and stalagmites which, tinted by minerals in the limestone, produce a fascinating, iridescent glow.*

Everglades

No other natural area in the National Park System, and perhaps the whole of the United States, is so delicately balanced between survival and destruction as the Everglades of Florida. And yet it has been abused by man and man's follies more than any other. Some speculate that if we ever lose a national park, it will probably be the Everglades, not through development — the boundaries are firmly fixed and the land protected from the bulldozer forever — but from the steady tipping of the ecological scales.

The Everglades is a broad, flat river of fresh water that flows from Lake Okeechobee in central Florida 120 miles south to Florida Bay and the Gulf of Mexico. It has done so since time unknown, an endless "river of grass" that moves so imperceptibly slowly it seems to stand still.

The Everglades is a certain kind of magic. Both ugly and beautiful, this magic — a sense of mystery and discovery — transcends the absolutes, the complexities, the disjointed and calamitous events that nearly destroyed and still threatens. Here is a tropical life blended with the temperate climate zone, where the nature of the mid-Atlantic states meets the species of the Caribbean in a rare setting of conflicts and contrasts.

A young alligator basks in the Florida sun below. *Alligators are a more common sight nowadays, lurking in and around the waters that also provide a home for numerous other creatures.*

The Cypress Mangrove Swamp, Tamiami Trail right *is part of the heritage of Everglades National Park, where all kinds of wildlife and endangered species thrive in a delicate ecological balance.*

Everglades

Once endangered, the alligator is making a comeback in Everglades; some species, however, have not been so fortunate and many birds and animals will never be seen again. The limpkin above right *and blue heron* above *are pictured among the delicate reeds which grow profusely in Everglades; other examples of the Park's vegetation are the water hyacinths* below.

Glacier

The towering majesty and grandeur of Glacier National Park is not all ours. We share it with Canada where the northern extension of Glacier Range in Alberta is Waterton Lake National Park. Together the two form the Waterton-Glacier International Peace Park, authorized and established in 1932 by the United States Congress and the Canadian Parliament as "a symbol of permanent peace and friendship".

The mountains of Glacier National Park are a part of the Rockies, that upheaval of mountain building that began about 75 billion years ago and extended in distance from South America through Mexico and the United States and Canada into Alaska and the Aleutians.

Glacier is the only area south of the Canadian border with a subarctic climate, and the plant and animal life reflect that. What was here prior to the ice age, if anything, is unknown for the glaciers virtually denuded the mountains of any fossils; but despite the deceiving barren-like appearance of the mountains, the park is a true wilderness, an ideal setting for a wide variety of wildlife and plants.

The glorious terrain of Glacier National Park stretches for mile after mile of symmetrical peaks, towering over jewel-like lakes. Exquisite flowers blossom here, like queencup left, *and glacier lilies opposite page bottom, which form a carpet against the backdrop of Mount Clements.*

The craggy pinnacles of Grinnel Point and Mount Gould are pictured behind Swiftcurrent Lake below; right are Mount Oberlin and Mount Cannon.

Set against the perfect azure of St. Mary Lake is Citadel Mountain; snow-covered slopes in the range behind contrast with the bleak gray of the mountain's face above.

Glacier

Set amid Glacier's unparalleled mountain scenery—magnificent mountains that are carved out of some of the oldest exposed rocks on the earth's surface—are some two hundred lakes, many of which are of glacial origin. These, and the myriad waterfalls, provide the visitor with scenes of breathtaking beauty, and an aura of peace and tranquillity.

Grand Canyon

Nothing, not the camera, the canvas, or the poet, will prepare you for what may be the greatest visual shock man can experience: your first view of the Grand Canyon. President Theodore Roosevelt in 1908 established the Grand Canyon as a national monument; by 1919 the Congress created the Grand Canyon National Park.

For nearly a century now we have pieced together an astounding story of earth erosion and upheaval spanning two billion years of the earth's existence. All we really know is that it is the Colorado River, still flowing and still carving, that has changed this land.

The Colorado begins in the Rocky Mountains and runs 1,450 miles to the Gulf of California. Along the way it is met by dozens of tributaries, the major of which is the Green River rising from the Wind River Mountains of Wyoming. Totally, the Colorado and its tributaries drain a land area of 240,000 square miles, and it drops ten thousand feet over hundreds of rapids before it reaches the sea.

But is has not been the Colorado alone that has created this spectacle. There were great land upheavals, tiltings caused by pressures from beneath the earth, which caused the river to run faster and erode deeper.

The Colorado will go on grinding and the walls of the canyon will continue to retreat until someday, millions of years from now, only a lazy river will meander across a plain where once was this magnificent sight.

Thought by many to be one of the world's wonders, the Grand Canyon is so vast that its immensity can hardly be described to those who have not seen it. A human figure lends scale to the view of Mohave Point above; *the light and time of day add rich red and golden hues to the rocks* above left *and* below left.

Evening shadows lengthen over the Grand Canyon's south rim, seen right *at Mohave Point and* overleaf *from the majestic peaks of Hopi Point.*

Almost everywhere in the Grand Canyon there is something new of something old to be seen. A change of viewpoint brings a new perspective to the timeless landscape, until the sheer grandeur of it all becomes overwhelming.

Layer upon layer of stratified rock rises from the canyon floor, where the Colorado River, seen at Lee's Ferry left winds like a slender ribbon through one of nature's most awe-inspiring spectacles.

Grand Teton

Find a rock, preferably one broad at the bottom and jagged at the top. Holding it by the bottom, push it deep into a pile of loose dirt until both the rock and your hand are covered. Then smooth the dirt to a flat surface. Now, slowly, with the jagged tip up, push the rock vertically, but leaning a little to the left, out of the dirt.

Not very scientific and perhaps a little messy, but this will offer some idea of what happened to the Grand Teton mountains.

Once upon a time the land all around this section of Wyoming and Idaho was flat, probably the bed of an ancient ocean. This past is so dim that scientists can only guess at sixty-five million or so years. It was during what they call the Laramide Revolution that things began to happen. As the Rocky Mountains were going through their pangs of birth, the movement below the earth's crust caused a great crack forty miles long and fifteen miles wide. Far below, where for a billion years molten lava had solidified into granite, the rock began to push up. As it did it leaned slightly to the west.

The great mountains of the Teton range are a virtual showcase of nature. The background changes almost daily, but the creatures that roam from the valley floor to the most remote peaks are the same. The elk has flourished. Each winter there are more than eight thousand. The moose, mule deer, black bear, bighorn sheep, beaver, weasel and the coyote, are well protected; even the grizzly, though it is seldom seen.

The wonders of the Tetons are many but their ravishing beauty will never reveal the tortuous events of their birth....

The saw-toothed Grand Teton mountain range these pages *began as a gigantic fault block uplifted from the earth's crust. Sculptured by streams and glaciers, these spectacular peaks now form a chain of pyramids, soaring more than a mile above the sagebush flats and lakes of Jackson Hole.*

The highest peak of the range, Grand Teton left, rises to a height of 13,747 feet above sea level, dominating the horizon.

The serrated peaks form a magnificent backdrop for the brush-covered flats of Jackson Hole overleaf.

Grand Teton

Set among the Grand Teton mountains, Jackson Lake shimmers in the morning light *far right*, *glistens at twilight* left, *and glows in spectacular sunsets* right *and* bottom right. *The lake was formed in a deep groove left by a piedmont glacier which passed through Jackson Hole during the first Ice Age.*

Some of the glaciers which gave the range its present form still remain and frigid glacial lakes dot the landscape.

Golden-leaved aspen trees below *enhance the jagged peaks of the Grand Teton.*

Great Smoky Mountains

The Great Smoky Mountains may be the oldest continuously inhabited area of the country. There was no great drought or violent volcanic eruptions to drive this civilization away. They hunted and farmed and thrived in what must surely have been their "Garden of Eden". But, alas, as years went by, the Cherokee one of the largest and most stable of America's early societies, was nearly destroyed and *Shaconage*, "the place of the blue smoke", their home for at least a thousand years of recorded time, nearly lost.

The Appalachians are about 400 million years old. No one knows precisely when the first plants and trees began to root but it was sometime after the last glacial period. All of that time plotted on the face of a rule stretches nearly to the end. The tragedies of the Smokies came in the last fraction of an inch, between the early 1800's and 1940 when the Great Smoky Mountain National Park was established.

The Great Smoky Mountains are a metaphor for nature. The park's 522,000 acres is seventy-five percent wilderness; its 800 miles of trails, 700 miles of streams, and sixteen peaks of over 6,000 feet are a paradise for those who love nature. And they come every year, nine million strong. This is the most visited of all national parks.

To find real peace of mind, it would be hard to better the soothing, calming effect of water as it tumbles and flows over falls, makes its way over and around rocks and boulders, or between the tree-lined banks of rivers and streams, of which there are several hundred miles in the Great Smoky Mountains National Park.

Grotto Falls below is one of the most beautiful in the park, reached by an easy hike of over two miles along the Nature Trail, through delightful scenery.

There are many vantage points from which to view the ever-changing and varied aspects of the Rocky Mountains. Top left *the view from Chimney Tops;* below *from Blue Ridge Parkway. The frothy, tumbling waters of the Little River are shown* above, *and* bottom left *a view of Oconaluftee River, near the park's entrance. This tranquil scene* right *is of Cades Cove.*

Hawaii Volcanoes and Haleakala

Hawaii is a living laboratory, one of the few places in the world where the layman, side-by-side with the scientist, watches and shares in the knowledge that all is not yet done. Steam breaks from tiny crevices in the rock, volcanic fire surges into the air from active vents, molten lava streaks down mountain flanks, and the earth trembles and thunders as the island interior moves, settles, and moves again in a constant process of building and reshaping.

Hawaii, the largest of the eight major islands in the chain, is almost hypnotic in its serenity and beauty — yet hanging over all of this is an awesome force of pent-up energy that man cannot reckon with. The visitor to Hawaii Volcanoes National Park witnesses the most spectacular of nature's forces.

Off to the northwest, and within sight of Hawaii, is Maui, which began as two volcanoes eventually joined by a bridge of land between them. The largest of the two mountains is Haleakala, "House of the Sun", twelve thousand feet above sea level. This is Haleakala National Park. Last active in 1790, earthquake records indicate that while there is still some adjustment taking place beneath, it is not likely ever to erupt again. But no one really knows. The scenery is the most striking on the Hawaiian Islands and is both beautiful and bizarre: Mark Twain described it as "The sublimest spectacle I ever witnessed…."

The native kupaoa, one of the few plants able to survive the desert-like conditions, clings tenaciously within the bowl of Haleakala Crater below.

The volcanic mountain Kilauea right last erupted in 1974. Its crater is filled with sulphur gases which issue from the Halemaumau firepit.

Many of the lava flows from Hawaii's volcanoes reach the coast where strange formations occur right. Despite the blanketing effect of the lava lichens, ferns and grasses soon grow again.

The exotic silversword plant below flowers for one week only, after many years of growth. Its beautiful blossoms of vivid purple and yellow fade, and the plant dies. New plants will form from the seeds dropped, and, in many years' time, will flower again. Half a mile of boardwalk on top of cinders and through a skeleton forest leads through Hawaii Volcano's aptly-named Devastation Trail overleaf.

Kings Canyon and Sequoia

The Sequoia — Giant Sequoia, Sierra redwood, *Sequoiadendron giganteum* — it makes little difference; it's still the big tree. It is "a species of the genus", which is another way of saying that it's in a class by itself, the largest living thing on earth. There are cousins, the taller, coastal redwoods, and the Douglas firs soar higher, but for sheer volume the Sequoia is one of a kind. For example, the General Sherman, discovered in 1879 by trapper James Wolverton and named for his Civil War commander, is estimated to be 2.5 thousand years old and may well be older. It is 272 feet tall — more than 100 feet higher than Niagara falls — and has a trunk diameter of 36 feet. And if that's not enough, its first limb, which just recently fell, was 130 feet from the ground and measured 7 feet in diameter.

The one most responsible for Sequoia National Park was John Muir, an enormously energetic man whose passion for the Sierra Nevada put much of this land into the protective custody of state and federal governments.

Called by the Spaniards "The River of the Holy Kings", the white-foamed water of Kings River descends through the rocky gorges at an incredible velocity opposite page bottom. In muted grandeur, the jagged peaks of the Sierra Nevada these pages command Kings Canyon. The flowering Yucca top right is just one of the many exotic species of plant found in the ever-changing scenery of Kings Canyon National Park.

Above *can be seen the parched summer-brown hillsides of Horseshoe Bend, a bleak backdrop to the waxy-white blooms of the flowering Yucca.* Right *Rock-climbers perch beside the pounding waters of Roaring River Falls in the cliff-dominated valley of Cedar Grove.*

Far right *The dramatic skies enhance the eerily-lit foreground, one of the many and varied scenes to be found in Kings Canyon National Park.*

Like a narrow ribbon above, the South Fork of the Kings River threads its way between precipitous canyon walls. You can almost hear these torrents of water left crashing down the granite walls of Grizzly Falls near Cedar Grove.

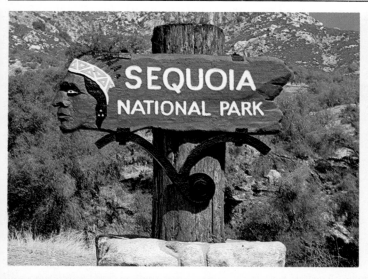

The majestic giant sequoia left *soars skywards, the survivor of an ancient lineage of huge trees. It is impossible to stand at the foot of such a tree without experiencing a surge of emotion. The size of these trees is* clearly illustrated above *by Tunnel Log, easily large enough for vehicles to pass through!*

Top right *is shown a stately group of sequoias in the Parker Group while* center right *is Resurrection Tree on Big Stump Nature Trail, and* right *Spring Tree in Grant Grove, which fell in 1931.*

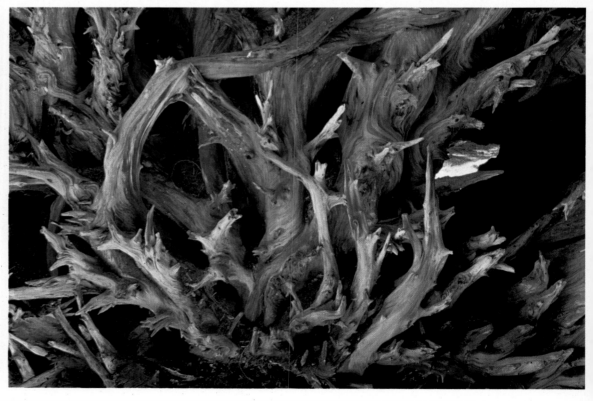

The Parker Group of giant sequoias
this page top *glows warmly in
dappled sunlight, while another
grand group is the Senate Group in
Giant Forest* above. *On the Congress
Trail can be found the gnarled roots
of Bear Den* right.

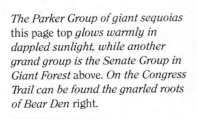

Shown left is the fire-ravaged trunk of the appropriately-named Burnt Monarch. The scene below is taken on the trail to Misty Falls along South Fork.

Left is shown the gnarled stump of a giant sequoia in Big Stump Basin—the smallness of the girl emphasises the enormity of these giants.

Below is the pretty little face of the distinctive yellow flower, black-eyed Susan.

Lassen Volcanic

If Lassen Peak ever erupts again it will take us all by surprise. But then, that is what Californians thought in May 1914. Lassen looked much like the other volcanoes in the Cascade Range: snowcapped, quiet, asleep; and no one, least of all President William Howard Taft, who proclaimed it a national monument, suspected life beneath the surface.

Directly south of the Peak is a basin of steam vents, hot springs, and mudpots, not unlike the thermal areas at Yellowstone. Nowadays it's called Bumpass Hell, named after a man who fell through the earth's thin crust into a mudpot, in 1865 and lived to talk about it.

Today you can climb through its perpetual snow to Lassen Peak and look into the crater, but down below, the mudpots continue to boil, and steam and gases hiss through the earth's cracks.

Lassen became a national park in 1916. The boundaries include 167 square miles of timberland, wildlife, several dozen fine lakes, and 300 species of wildflowers, all of which, it must be assumed, live on borrowed time. Lassen is a small park, as wilderness areas go, but to the climber and skier it is a charming bit of primitive landscape.

The scenes pictured these pages *and* overleaf *capture the excitement of Lassen Volcanic National Park.* Left *is a walkway in Little Hot Springs Valley, while the seething mud-pots, hissing hot springs, bubbling fumaroles and barren volcanic landscapes* below, right, *and below* right *can all be seen in Lassen's own moon-scape—Bumpass Hell.*

Overleaf *is shown the aptly named Chaos Crags.*

In 1914, Lassen Peak started to erupt culminating, in 1915, in a massive expulsion of vapor, ashes and lava. Eruptions continued, though on a decreasing scale, until 1917. The visitor to the area above can today see stunning evidence of nature's power, both past and present.

Lassen Volcanic National Park is surely a delight to every photographer, both amateur and professional, as it offers such an immense variety of scenery. Left is tranquil Manzanita Lake while right is the serene, tree-rimmed Hat Lake.

Part of Lassen's Bumpass Hell, with its self-guiding nature-trail and diversified hydrothermal area, is shown above. South east of Lassen Peak lie Kings Creek Meadows where the crystal waters of Kings Creek snake tortuously towards these gigantic stair-steps left and sparkling falls.

Mammoth Cave

Some 240 million years ago, the seas that covered what is now west-central Kentucky deposited layer-upon-layer of mud, shells, and sand. All of these hardened into the limestone and sandstone we see today. Then as the land around uplifted, the seas drained away, seeping through cracks in the earth's crust and eroding away the underground stone. Millions of years of this abrasive action created hundreds of caves and passageways, and from the ceilings, where the ground-water has percolated through, myriad colorful stalactites.

One hundred and fifty miles of Mammoth Cave have been explored, and speleologists, that marvelous breed of underground enthusiasts, believe that there may be hundreds more that link this great system to others in this section of the country. The most sought-after and challenging connection was made in 1972 when the Mammoth and nearby Flint Ridge Cave systems were linked by a spunky team of five people who, after a night of some of the most difficult caving, discovered a previously unsurveyed route.

Scenes from Mammoth Cave National Park are illustrated these pages. Left is shown one of the park's features, the limestone bluffs, but the park's main attraction is undoubtedly its incredible network of caves.

Below is shown Thorp's Pit; opposite page top is known as Kentucky Avenue and opposite page bottom, Roaring River.
(National Park Service Photos)

Mesa Verde

Mesa Verde, the "green table" in Spanish, is but a small part of the Colorado Plateau, the drainage basin of the Colorado River, typified by high mesas and deep canyons. Early Americans came here some ten thousand years ago, no doubt by the frozen Aleutian link to Asia. Today man attempts to devise some pattern of life for this nomad. Although each little bone, bit of ash, and piece of carved stone offers a clue, the puzzle is still fragmented. Part lies in Mexico and Peru, part is scattered across the northern and eastern United States, and part lies here in this little corner of Colorado. To be sure, the Americans separated as they traveled south from Alaska. Some found a route farther south and established great civilizations. Some moved east and north and became the American Indian we know best, and who survived the longest. Others moved to the sea and the southern California and Baja peninsula, and barely existed. Those that stayed here seem to have remained for a period of about eight hundred years. Exactly why they left is the mystery that surrounds this place and has baffled archeologists for years.

That these cliff dwellers left, and left en masse, for other parts is a certainty. Whatever the reason, the quest for survival led them elsewhere. Search as we may, clues to the exodus of these people elude us, but we do not lack evidence of their life here. Spruce Tree House, for example, has been marvelously preserved. There are 114 living rooms and eight ceremonial rooms to this apartment complex, and each has offered a tiny bit of information on how the people lived and worked and played,

A multitude of prehistoric ruins can be found in the fascinating Mesa Verde (literally "green table") National Park which rises high above the Mancos Valley. Towards the end of the 12th century the Indians, who lived in well-made stone houses on the Mesa tops, moved down to the cliff-face caves these pages. Nobody knows exactly why they did this, nor why, at the end of the 13th century, these dwellings too were suddenly abandoned, leaving them much as we find them today.

Mount McKinley

"Mount McKinley is the highest peak on the North American continent, 20,300 feet, and may well be the highest mountain in the world from its true base." If that were all there is to say about this magnificent national park, it would be quite enough, for of all the great Alaskan landscape, Mount McKinley is by far the most spectacular. But there is much more to this geologically significant land, for here is our link to the great glacial age that sculpted so much of the Northern Hemisphere. Mount McKinley sits in a sea of ice floes that, to this day, slowly transforms this northern outpost of the long chain of mountains that runs from South America, through the United States and Canada, on to the Aleutians.

The 600-mile Alaska Range, of which McKinley stands tallest, is the interface of the largest crustal break of North America, the Denali Fault System, where, millions of years ago, two great land masses met and folded together, one being pushed deep into the earth, the other raised to great heights.

The scenery is spectacular, and the wildlife — the grizzly, caribou, Dall sheep, moose, and all — is magnificent. It seems at first glance that nothing at Mount McKinley, in all of Alaska, could be wrong, that this is a place where everything is all right with God and the world.

Above the ragged summits and glacier-strewn valleys bottom left *gleaming Denali, as the Athabaskans called this 16,000 foot mountain, presides benignly, its massive bulk seen from Mount Healy* below, *reflected in the tundra pond* right, *and dwarfing the shuttle bus that perches at its base* left.

(Photo *below:* Fred Hirschmann; all other photos: National Parks Service).

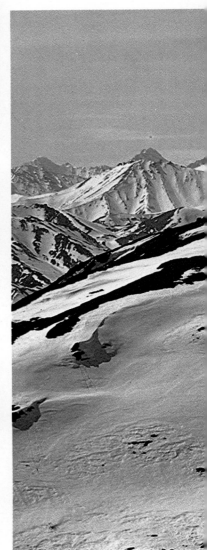

Mount McKinley—remote and enigmatic—is seen opposite page top left *in mid-summer across a cottongrass-lined taiga pond.* Opposite page top right *is one of the mountain's awe-inspiring, river-like glaciers.*

Despite the seemingly inhospitable surroundings, Mount McKinley National Park plays host to a fascinating array of wildlife including the grizzly bear left, *the boreal owl* right, *and the caribou* above. *These and many other species share their habitat in an enduring, if delicate balance—and it is the harsh winter that poses the greatest challenge to survival. Most of the birds migrate to the warmer south during the cold months, and the little ground squirrel hibernates. Of those animals which stay for the winter, one useful adaptation is the exchange of summer to winter coats.*

Mount Rainier

Mount Rainier is like a beckoning signal. "Come. I challenge you", it says. It dominates the sky of northwest Washington. On a clear day, within a one hundred mile radius, the peak of Rainier is never out of sight. Fly south to San Francisco from Seattle and the pilot reverently tips his wings in salute. Off to the left at sunset Rainier is a golden dome, sometimes hovering over the landscape, sometimes peeking above the clouds.

Rainier's glaciers are one of the park's main features, although the term "feature" seems hardly dignified for this grand old mountain. Nonetheless, scientists study them, climbers cross them to get to the summit, and casual visitors can drive near them. The Emmons Glacier is the largest; five miles long and one mile wide. There are twenty-seven named rivers of ice on the mountain covering about forty square miles. Nearly half of them originate on or near the summit, and each slowly works its way down the slopes, pushing before it and dragging beneath it tons of rocky debris that continues to shape and form the Mount Rainier of the future.

Like the glaciers of Glacier National Park, the glaciers here have diminished considerably in the past century, but there is still time. And like the volcanic chambers beneath the snows, life may yet be renewed. No law of nature has been found yet that will accurately forecast the next ice age or the next violent eruption.

Rainier casts a spell. Those who climb it, hike the trails, or simply drive or fly within its shadow can never forget the experience. A veteran mountaineer described it this way:

"Mount Rainier has been and continues to be to me the 'standard' for the 'good life.' Over the last 30 years I have found peace, health, happiness, comradeship, humility, and patience in scrambling over its ridges and glaciers and climbing to its crest. In contrast to the asphalt and concrete of man's cities, this pile of lava and ice has satisfied and stimulated all my senses. The experiences and memories founded on this mountain are endless...."

Anyone can benefit from the influence of the mountain. After a few days high on the rock and snow, all of one's faculties are sharpened. The meadows are so green, the flowers so colorful and the flowing streams so sweet as one descends from the barren world above. There is no room left here for petty worries, depression, or negative thoughts — one is reoriented. Man is as he should be.

Beautiful Mount Rainier stands 12,500 feet above flower-filled valleys, these pages.

Ribbons of crystal water cascade down Falls Creek *left while* below Yakima Peak is seen from Ricksecker Point. Mount Rainier reigns supreme *right beneath a cloudless blue sky across Paradise, and* above *is seen the scenic splendor of pine-circled Bench Lake.*

The entrancing view overleaf *shows Mount Rainier softly clothed in romantic mist beyond Paradise Point.*

Olympic

Olympic National Park is a rain forest; it is a lofty mountain, millions of years old; it is a stretch of nearly virgin Pacific coastline; it is a classic wilderness with wild rivers and streams, alpine lakes and meadows, a host of animal life, one thousand species of plants, and tall trees…

It begins along a fifty mile section of rugged coast where trees grow on the very edge of the Pacific Ocean and where the life-giving water cycle that *is* Olympic has its start and end. This islanded and rocky strip of beach along Washington's Pacific shore is one of the most primitive sections of seacoast yet remaining in the United States. Here is the great Olympic Rain Forest, a luxuriously green woodland that rivals any tropical jungle for beauty and wildlife — an environment unto itself where trees a thousand years old survey the world from three hundred feet and shield a carpet of dense moss and ferns.

Olympic became a national monument in 1909. In 1938 it was enlarged and designated a national park. In 1953 the coastal area was added; now it contains in all 900 thousand acres.

Olympic National Park these pages and overleaf, *has something for everyone, whether it be boating on a beautiful lake* left, *swimming* right *or wandering amid breathtakingly beautiful scenery.*

Gathering dusk enfolds the sculptured peaks of the Olympic Range, seen beyond dense stands of conifers below, *and beyond the burnished waters of Great Bend on Hood Canal* left. *Below left is a dreamy view of Crescent Lake.*

Olympic

Contained between Hood Canal to the east and the mighty Pacific Ocean to the west, Olympic is a scenic wilderness.

Sunset seems to flood the boatmen at Great Bend on Hood Canal right. *The beauty of Lake Crescent is captured in this entrancing photograph* left.

Olympic National Park boasts some 50 miles of unspoiled ocean coastline where bleached driftwood lines the sandy shore below.

Petrified Forest

The 148 square miles of land that now form Petrified Forest National Park are like a giant jewel box. There is the mystery of what Freeman Tilden called "The Forest That Was", made all the more mysterious by the mere fact that, try as one may, the eye finds absolutely no clue to the once tropical jungle of lush, exotic vegetation, lakes, and swamps, animal life unknown today, and abundant rainfall that once was here. This is the desert, and a desert it has been for millions of years. No clue at all; that is unless you look closely.

Strewn across this barren, forbidding landscape are trees — well, they look like trees; occasionally one will have roots, and on some the bark appears to have been preserved. But they are no longer upright and they are stone, stone hard enough to scratch all but the toughest of metals. Once they were giant conifers, not unlike some that still grow in South America. There were ferns and cycads and dozens of other plants. The land was flat, probably at about sea level and, according to the Plate Tectonics theory, about 1,700 miles closer to the equator, and roaming around all this was a collection of giant amphibious reptiles. This was 200 million years ago. All of these things are still there — trees and ferns and animals…fossilized.

The beautiful landscapes in the park include the Tepees top left, small peaks resembling tepees or haystacks showing erosion of soft, layered clay deposits; and the Blue Mesa left and above.

Arizona's Petrified Forest is unique among the petrifications of the world in its size, variety and scope. The transition from tree to stone has been so gradual and perfect that every detail, each minute fiber, is completely preserved. Right is shown an example of a petrified log.

Lee's Ferry above left, *named after one of Utah's great pioneers, marks the point at which the mighty Colorado River issues from shadow into brief sunlight before plunging again into chasms of its own carving. The varying bands of color representing the different rock types can be seen* above *around the hills of the Blue Mesa.*

The Painted Desert opposite page top *and* bottom, *and* left *provides the beholder with spectacular panoramas of strange and exotic landscapes, whose colors change as the direction and intensity of light alters. The Painted Desert was so named by Spanish explorers because of the brilliant colors of its waterless plateaux, buttes and mesas.*

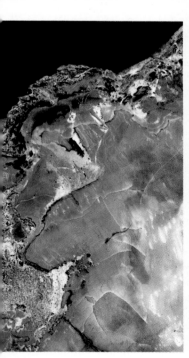

Redwood

Redwood National Park came about in 1968, only after the most ferocious battles with the lumber industry. Only about sixty-two thousand acres are now protected by the National Park Service, and nearly half of that is actually state park land.

The tallest trees are along Redwood Creek where Dr. Zahl found his prize. Protected though they may be from the saw, continued cutting on slopes and ridgetops nearby threatens to simply wash them away.

Once found in many parts of the world — Canada, England, Western Europe — the redwoods depend on ocean-created climates of moderate year-round temperatures and thick summer fogs. Here along the northern California coast they thrive in pure stands as well as in mixed forests with maples, cedar, and alder.

Call them what you will, interpret their mood as you will, they stand as sentinels of the nation. The California coast redwood was here long before Western man knew of this hemisphere and, no doubt, now that its boundaries are secured, some of them, at least, will be here long after us.

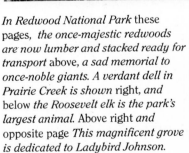

In Redwood National Park these pages, *the once-majestic redwoods are now lumber and stacked ready for transport* above, *a sad memorial to once-noble giants. A verdant dell in Prairie Creek is shown* right, *and* below *the Roosevelt elk is the park's largest animal.* Above right *and* opposite page *This magnificent grove is dedicated to Ladybird Johnson.*

Rocky Mountain

The Rockies are a part of a much larger system of mountains in the western hemisphere, the cordillera (Spanish, meaning chain of mountains), as it is called, which extends from Argentina to Alaska. In North America this vast crustal disturbance is divided into sections: the Rockies, the Plateaus, the Basins and Ranges, the Sierra Nevada, the Cascades, and the Coast ranges. Within its own family these are the Southern or Colorado Rockies. The range in Wyoming is the Middle Rockies, in Idaho and Montana the Northern Rockies, and the Canadian Rockies.

At the center of the Southern Rockies is Rocky Mountain National Park, no less than 65 peaks rising above 10,000 feet, more than 400 square miles of virtually unspoiled nature and scenic splendor set aside by the federal government in 1915. It was a long time in preparing: some 300 million years ago, in fact, when the ancestral mountains began uplifting from the seas that covered the western United States. About 70 million years ago the last inland ocean drained away. This was the beginning of what we see now. For the next 60 to 65 million years there were alternating periods of volcanic activity, uplifting, and erosion. Then, some seven million years ago, there was a final broad uplift of the region.

Beautiful Bear Creek in Colorado's Rocky Mountain National Park is shown left. Shrouded in mist, Long's Peak, towering 14,255 feet high, dominates the skyline over Trail Ridge Road below.

Picturesque lakes stud the park's landscape such as Nymph Lake above left, *dammed by sunbleached tree trunks, and Dream Lake* above.

The beaver makes his home amid the tranquil scenery of Beaver Ponds, in Hidden Valley left, *while the ground squirrel* below *is surely one of the park's most charming residents.*

Overleaf *is an entrancing view of Dream Lake with Flattop Mountain in the background.*

Virgin Islands

Columbus discovered the tropical Virgin Islands on his second voyage in 1493 but, as seemed his luck, he was not the first; South American Indians had been there since 300 A.D. Their village remains and petroglyphs have been found scattered about St. John.

Although there were various claims on the islands during the next two hundred years, St. Thomas and St. John were not formally settled until the early-eighteenth century, and then by private, chartered companies that established sugar and cotton plantations.

The Virgin Islands are the tips of ancient sedimentary deposits and volcanic activity, and were formed much the same as other areas in the national parks. Even here the theories of plate tectonics and the moving of the earth's crust over explosive funnels in the core beneath, explains much of the land construction.

Virgin Islands National Park is on what some call the heavenly side of St. John, where the trade winds and sparkling waters bring fantasies of pirates and buccaneers, where man's conflict with nature is washed fresh by the unspoiled sea, and where the solitude of a visit renews one's communication with the outside world.

One of the most beautiful places in the world is surely Virgin Islands National Park *these pages. Crystal clear, azure-blue waters characterize* Leinster Bay *left where can be found stunning coral reefs. White-gold sands line the shores of* Trunk Bay *above left situated on the north-west coast of the island.*

Virgin Islands National Park *boasts a beautiful and varied coastline, from the rugged splendor of* Salt Pond Bay *above, to the serene tranquillity of* Cinnamon Bay *right and below, or* Maho Bay *bottom right. Several species of cactus may be found here including the exotic* Turk's head *top right.*

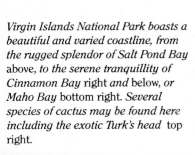

Yellowstone

Fortunately for all, the creation of Yellowstone as a preserve came before western land exploitation made its way into this high country, so we can only speculate what might have happened given another century. We know the wildlife was already endangered from hunting and trapping and remained so for a number of years after the park was formed. In fact some species were nearly destroyed from the mere lack of law enforcement. If gold had been discovered — and certainly it was sought — politics would have been a formidable force with which to reckon. As it is, Yellowstone National Park is nearly 3,500 square miles of virgin wilderness, land unchanged except by nature itself. Less than two percent of the total area has been affected by man's intrusion. Not only is it the nation's largest wildlife preserve, it is a geologic wonderland unlike any on earth: spouting geysers, bubbling mudpots, steaming fumaroles and pools of boiling water, hundreds of ponds and lakes surrounded by dense forests, rivers and streams rushing through black and yellow canyons…all this and much, much more.

Yellowstone is America's largest wildlife preserve and its environs provide the habitat for such creatures as the wapiti (elk) right, *bison* bottom and bottom right *and deer* below.

The Yellowstone River is dwarfed by sheer canyon walls of dark lava, thickly forested on either side of foaming falls, and at Lower Falls opposite page *it thunders down a breathtaking 308 feet, spreading foam and mist for a remarkable distance.*

Yellowstone

Castle Geyser left *and* right *is thought to be the oldest geyser in Yellowstone. Its unusual eruption is in two phases—first it spouts water for 30 minutes and then it steams noisily for more than an hour. The photograph* bottom left *shows the colored algal rings which encircle Grand Prismatic Spring, while* below *steaming water cascades into Firehole River.*

Overleaf is a superb photograph illustrating the gaunt skeletons of dead trees rising from the floor of Opalescent Pool.

Minerva Terrace center left *illustrates the fact that geological action has resulted in surface cave-like formations. The terrace is located in Yellowstone's famous Mammoth Hot Springs where terraces of travertine were created by a form of calcium carbonate, dissolved from the limestone beneath the ground, which was carried to the surface by hot water.*

West Thumb Geyser Basin on the shores of Yellowstone Lake is a small, concentrated area of lake shore geysers and hot springs of which Percolating Springs above are among its most spectacular features. Left is shown Grand Prismatic Spring, the park's largest.

Yosemite

To simply say that Yosemite Valley is beautiful beyond description is, in today's parlance, a "cop-out". The place moves everyone, without exception, and no one leaves without having been touched in some form.

El Capitan, the largest single block of granite on the earth, defies even the wildest imagination, yet it is poetry in itself. Its moods, like the walls of the Grand Canyon, change with the hour, the day, the season. Find it in the morning sun, or with slight traces of snow clinging to tiny ledges on its nearly sheer face, and you have an image indelible for life.

El Capitan's massiveness, and that of Half Dome, Glacier Point, and other mammoth peaks and pinnacles, is at first frightening; should they come crashing down in some cataclysmic earthquake, it would seem the world would end. Yet walk among them for awhile and they become giant guardians of the fragile life below in the valley, forever ensconced by the gods to watch over a paradise of more rapidly moving life cycles. Glaciers, mighty rivers of ice hundreds of feet thick, created Yosemite Valley and cut away the now weathered, polished face of Half Dome.

Yosemite National Park has countless attractions which draw many visitors all year round to admire its beautifully-preserved countryside. Amid Yosemite's grandiose mountains and groves of conifers tumble crystal clear waterfalls such as the thunderous torrent, *Vernal Fall* left. The dramatic cliffs of El Capitan are shown *below, and* above *their mighty bulk faces Cathedral Rocks and the shiny ribbon of Bridalveil Fall.*

Yosemite National Park comprises almost 1,200 square miles of varied scenery and breathtaking beauty. It was created principally when huge blocks of granite, formed beneath the earth's surface, were buckled and lifted by immense pressure. This was followed by glacial action which carved vast valleys and basins which eventually became lakes.

Bridalveil Fall is shown above and the mysteriously beautiful Cathedral Spires is seen right.

The massive grandeur of Cathedral Rocks can be seen left *while* above *the Upper and Lower Yosemite Falls leap spectacularly down the vertical rocks that rise dramatically from the valley floor.*

Overleaf: *The Merced River threads its way along the floor of the Yosemite Valley.*

At sunset, the polished face of Half Dome glows with an almost mystic iridescence *opposite page* *above the peaceful Merced River.* Half Dome is *seen* left *from Glacier Point.*

Atop Sentinel Dome, the gnarled and twisted Jeffrey Pine *below is seen in sharp relief at sunset* bottom.

Zion

When man clashes with nature, he leaves his mark. His creativity and destruction stand for centuries and, while ultimately it may be subdued, it may never be erased.

There is one thing man leaves behind that, in many ways, is revealing and, irrespective of the intrusion, offers something the instruments can never detect. The mark he makes on a map or the name he gives a place or thing can often tell more of the powerful struggle, the emotions, the pain and sorrow, and the joys and ecstasies of his discoveries than any computer yet devised. Such is the case in the vast country of Zion National Park, where the Mormon pioneers, seeking their ecclesiastical haven, found a certain peace and serenity. While their names for cliffs and domes and rugged canyons seem totally incongruous with the dramatic and massive forces of nature that created this place, the names stuck, and today we cannot help but agree with these people who articulated a vision. Zion itself means "the heavenly city of God". "Angel's Landing" and the "Great White Throne" at first glance look like anything but something God would have sanctioned, but this is what they saw, and who are we to dispute these temples, altars, and pulpits?

Zion is a land of "peace and comfort", as they said, but to the solely geological eye, it takes some time to piece together this handiwork of nature and find that kind of solitude. The past was less than harmonious. The elements clashed with the earth, as indeed they do still. Monolith after monolith in this park stand as mute testimony to millions of years erosion typical of southern Utah.

Zion Canyon, in Zion National Park, is a spectacular, multi-colored gorge, where giant stone masses such as the East Temple bottom left and below, and Lady Mountain right dominate the landscape. Left above is shown the familiar silhouette of the Temples and Towers of the Virgin.

From Canyon Overlook there are incredible panoramic views of the canyon overleaf.

Zion

Above shows Canyon Overlook where people gather to admire the spectacular views that the position affords.

Prominent top are the sheer walls of Angels Landing while right the strange markings of Checkerboard Mesa are the result of weathering along vertical and horizontal planes of weakness in the sandstone.

Above *is shown the huge bulk of the Sentinel across the waters of the North Fork of Virgin River while* left *is one of the many fascinating examples of crossbedded sandstone to be found in Zion National Park.*

Right *is pictured the graceful delicacy of the golden columbine while* overleaf *is the yellow snakeweed, a member of the sunflower family.*

Published by CHARTWELL BOOKS, INC. A division of BOOK SALES, INC.
110 Enterprise Avenue, Secaucus, New Jersey 07094
© 1981 Illustrations and text: Colour Library International Ltd., New Malden, Surrey, England.
Colour separations by FERCROM, Barcelona, Spain.
Display and text filmsetting by Focus Photoset & The Printed Word, London, England.
Printed by Cayfosa and bound by Eurobinder - Barcelona (Spain)
ISBN 0 89009-468-3